Nocturnal

This is an IndieMosh book

brought to you by MoshPit Publishing
an imprint of Mosher's Business Support Pty Ltd

PO Box 4363
Penrith NSW 2750

indiemosh.com.au

Copyright © Catherine Harford 2022

The moral right of the author has been asserted in accordance with the Copyright Amendment (Moral Rights) Act 2000.

All rights reserved. Except as permitted under the Australian Copyright Act 1968 (for example, fair dealing for the purposes of study, research, criticism or review) no part of this publication may be reproduced, stored in a retrieval system, or transmitted in any form or by any means, electronic, mechanical, photocopying, recording or otherwise, without the written permission of the publisher.

A catalogue record for this work is available from the National Library of Australia

https://www.nla.gov.au/collections

Title: Nocturnal

Subtitle: A Collection of Poems

Author: Harford, Catherine (1976–)

ISBN: 9781922812841 (paperback)

Subjects: POETRY/Australian & Oceanian; BODY, MIND, SPIRIT/Supernatural; PSYCHOLOGY/Mental Health FAMILY & RELATIONSHIPS/Bullying

No individual in these poems is taken from real life. Any resemblance to any person or persons living or dead is accidental and unintentional. The author, their agents and publishers cannot be held responsible for any claim otherwise and take no responsibility for any such coincidence.

Cover concept by Catherine Harford.
Cover design and layout by Ally Mosher at allymosher.com
Internal images by Catherine Harford.

Moontime Haunting

Also by Catherine Harford:

They Gave Me Truth
Under Moon and Sun
American Creek

NOCTURNAL

A COLLECTION OF POEMS

CATHERINE HARFORD

For Alecia
Which witch?
My favourite witch!
Thanks for all of the magic

Contents

INTRODUCTION 1

12 AM AND COUNTING

Nocturnal 7
- The Hurtling Planet 8
- Sold Out 9
- The Dedication 10
- The Devastator 12
- Try and Breathe 14
- The Wizard of Oz 16
- Love Heals All 18
- The Value in Art 22
- The Silver Bullet 23
- The Status Crisis 26
- Who Are You Again? 29
- Delusions of Grandeur 30
- Fone the Tone 32
- Ah, Tedium 33
- Let's Get It On 34
- Capitalism High 36
- There's No Money in Art 38
- Gentlemen Behaviour 39
- Lecture Me 40
- Real Men 41
- Show Us Your Tits 42

1 AM AND ALONE

The Exemption 47
- Donnie Darko Dissing 48

Malignant 50
Trolls 52
Summer Loving... 53
The Relevance of You............................... 56
The Twisted Abyss..................................... 58
Pathological Narcissists 59
The Foe 60
No Signal 64
My Chunky Life 65
Blue Beard 66
Decision Time 68
Ludicrous Expectations 70
Porn Brain... 71
Just Joshing... 72
Maiden, Witch and Crone 75
Anti-Christian 76
Lost Cause 78
The Hoax 80
Cut the Cord 82
Time Waster.. 83
A Cold War in the Global Village 84
War of Words 86

2 AM AND DANCING

My Way 89
The Highways and Byways of Life.................... 90
Ladies Don't Fart.. 94
The Matriarch 96
Waiting 97
State the Obvious 98
The Asp 99

Always Was, Always Will Be 100
Wild Woman 102
The Loved Ones 103
Terminal Happiness 104
Winter is Coming 105
The Bends 106
The Outskirts 108
Fuck Off, Ho 110
Only the Strange 112
The Time Has Come 114
Cellular Bomb-times 116
Bloom 117
Humble Pie 118
The Urban Addict 119
Close Your Eyes 120
The Frozen Heart 122
Denied 124
Hail the Greedy 125
Get Away 126
Don't Leave 127
The Devil Grins 128
Tempted to Hate 130
Potty Mouth 133

3 AM AND COMING HOME

The Call of Nature 137
Last Night 138
Men 139
The Shit Heap 140
The Chopper 142
Jealous Jeans 143

Love's a Peach	144
The Shallows	147
When the War Finally Ends	149
Time	150
The Takeaway	152
Portray	154
Black Dog Blues	155
The Smiling Assassin	166
Will You Marry Me?	168
Soul Man	170
Your Choice	171
Soul Doubt	172
The Tainted Ones	173
Stop, Thief	174
The Inbred Catastrophe	176
Bye Bye Baby	178
I Said No	179
Strange Bedfellows	180
Weirdo	182
Guns Are Fucked (But Not as Fucked as the Assholes That Kill People With Them)	183
The Expert	188
ACKNOWLEDGEMENTS	190
ABOUT THE AUTHOR	193

Introduction

Nocturnal is my third collection of poetry, which is not to say it's my most recent work. Rather, it is the work I have found to harbour an edgier flavour, a grittier content, a lot more swear words and frankly, a whole lot more sex than I would tend to include in my poems.

It's not as though I felt the need to exclude this adult content from my other collections – it's more so that I sensed that I wanted to create a space for them to come into the world together, where they might complement one another, and speak to a certain theme of living that does little to shy away from the darker side of existence.

Undoubtedly as you read through this work, I imagine it becomes obvious that I have dealt with a lot of mental health issues in my adult life. If you have read my book, "They Gave Me Truth" you will have certain insight into what I mean when I say this. To be honest, I have kept a great deal of that which brought on my depression, anxiety and C-PTSD to myself –

I just have no desire to make public that which has caused me the deepest distress in my life. The convoluted psychological anguish I suffered in my youth, unfortunately at the hands of those I loved the most in this world, is something I prefer to keep to myself, and spare any more hurt for those that I know were hurting so greatly when they hurt me.

As I moved on in life and tried to heal from this childhood trauma, I found myself unwittingly at the mercy of others in my new world who made it their mission to make my life a living hell. They're not my family, so they're fair game. Let's face it, a writer needs fodder, obviously, but the fact also becomes that if you are isolated in a community that is not yours, and you are bullied mercilessly, where do you put those realities?

I desperately needed to process the awful taunting I was subjected to, and I did it in the place, the space where I felt I could do it the most justice. I knew that I was experiencing this torment for a reason, and what appeared to my bullies as my weakness in keeping my mouth shut, was truthfully me running into my world of words to process their actions and make some strange sense of what seemed like a maniacal kind of senselessness. To this end, I really need show no mercy, because they really did pick the wrong target – I may have seemed voiceless and weak to them, oh dear, it turns out I'm anything but!

On this journey, I discovered Pathological Narcissism, I discovered Christian Psychopathy, I discovered the Golden Loop and the strange, cutthroat reality that drives everyday people to the brink when they are shovelled together in a crammed city that barely sees them, let alone meets their soul needs. I learned all of this, and so of course, I want to share that insight. If my work is somehow able to alleviate for others the confusion that comes from dealing with an incessant, shameless bully who shows no mercy in the face of their own twisted realities, it's well worth it.

So here in this book, the night prowler emerges. The hungry beast that lurches and dances deep into the night, seeking lust and love and life. In the witching hour, the hurts find momentum and hit hard, but likewise, the knowing, the wisdom behind it all, the lessons that were meant to be learnt step out of the shadows and demand to be felt. There is so much depth in life, and the darkness carries as much weight in living a full life as what the light does. But not everyone is brave enough to open their eyes when the light is turned off.

The night is the time for contemplation, for satisfying desires, for dancing through the fire and soaking up the starlight. Some of us seek it, we hunt for it, we need it – we are nocturnal.

Catherine Harford, 2022

12 AM AND COUNTING

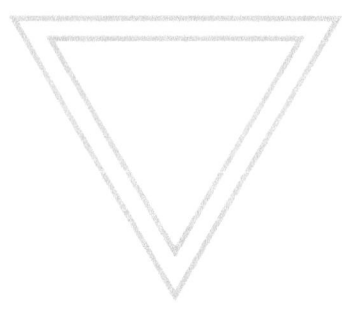

Nocturnal

At the back of midnight
In the witching hour
Shadows fall

The Hurtling Planet

Driving through the fog
Picking up glinting eyes
In high beams

Night seems special
In a race to the finish line
Decking out the pavement

Kilometres stretch
Moving us
From one town to the next

The human arrangement
Vehicular estrangement
In a moonlight so bold

It calms the lurching spirit
Hurtling along the highways
Of a hurtling planet

Motionless
Kept steady
By the ease of navigation

Sold Out

> There's a fine line
> Between selling your soul
> And having a soul
> That's worth selling

The Dedication

Who are you kidding?
You think I chanced upon this?

You'll never see
The time spent in worship
On my knees
Giving all
To a god
Whose will
Is such
You'll never believe
Without a dream
An itch to scratch
Love and despatch

You'll need to want it
Hardcore despondent
No less
Society's best

A jovial divulgence of shit

But you must look past
And see it

Just another demand?
Or a testament drawn in the
        sand?
Craving fixtures of truth
And resonance

Colour energy explosion
The state of transportation
Oscillating rhythms
Passed on through timeframes

Just one taste
And you'll never be the same

The Devastator

Tsk, tsk, tsk

Now who ever said
That would pay off?

The dream, again
The dream
Who perpetuated
That dream?

Who screamed discontent
An aggressively passive way
A passage for this will sent
The flurry, the furore
Of the newer day

Who said it, hey?

The black phase
Of a new stick
A big dick
And you cling to your story

Your morning fucking glory

Don't tell me I didn't design this plan
You are who I am
Devastating to the core

Be myself around you?
What the hell for?

Try and Breathe

Sweet, blessed relief
Is there a wave of thought
In this adult communication?

Can't be the truth
Too much face to save
Why delve into a deep space?
Sandy bottoms should be seen
Close to the floor

Besides, it's not about you
Not really

High self-esteem
Reeling into obsession
And the need to talk shit

But to make light of it
To suggest it's normal
To pass over so easily on your
         feelings?

No one wants to hear it
It really is disturbing

How can I express my truths?
There's no way of knowing
No time for proving
Determining

Your pungent overlay
Of self-procured needs
Where everyone else is the fool

Hold on
And brave the tempered storm
Relief should be a few breaths
      away

Take a few short breaths
Try and breathe freely

The Wizard of Oz

A picture
A notion of reality
That fits into a scheme
Or a scene
That plays itself out
Without the interference
Of a shot-by-shot breakdown

Break it down
Breaking it down
With every piece of dialogue
That escapes

How do you behave normally
When your subtle reality
Is the almighty Oz

But you're just that frail little man
                or woman
Behind the curtain
Trying desperately
To push and pull
All the buttons and levers

Blowing out smoke screens
Booming voice operations
Working overtime
To keep up the illusion
Of grandeur

Trying so hard
To be fraudulently profound
In these moments that present
               themselves
Under the guise
Of normality

These character interplays

Acting your arse off
Because no one bothered
To peak their head around
Behind the curtain
And calmly tell you
It isn't real

Love Heals All

The consortium of a memory
That flows through
An axiom of time
Like a demanding lover
May just fluke it
And hit its mark

Mmmm, the sweet spot

Contempt flurries
As the sudden onset
Familiarity of touch
Of arousal
Of spousal dynamic
Intrigues the flow of warmth
Like a dragline of desire
The gravitational-like pull
Welling up between thighs
Between soul space and
          heartbeats

Retreating into
The folds of flesh
Heady aromas
Steady needs
As the burning subterfuge
Of heavy hearts
Evaporates

Pictures of pesthouses
Fritter away
As the underscore of longing
Comes dancing into
The parselene lightness
Of a poorly lit room

The touches
The moans
The groans for more, more
Don't stop
The licking
The squelching
The slapping of thighs
The liberating of stars
Glittering the night skies

Petals unfurl
A whirlwind of sensation
Tagging all of the times
This love was made before

The ghost of petit larceny
Of young lovers stealing moments
Offering glimpses
Stashing nought
But distant memories

Stoushing over game plays
The insistence of insight
Rewarded handsomely
On the journey undertaken
To go deeper

Merely a pettifogging
Of tumbling tableaux

Merely the culmination
Of the long haul
As legs and hearts
Are thrust wide open
To receive it all
So wild and free

The deeply fissured bark
Of the family tree

Escaping together
Tasting the cream
Reviving the dream
That kept

Tears for humanity wept
Allow sorbefacient lust
To work its sorcery

The magic made
The second coming
The succumb to fitful sleep

Held in the arms of love
And the light that lingers there

The Value in Art

Shitting on the birth of creativity

Listen to me
Listen to me, why not?

Save yourself
From the mundane side
Of your brain

And the holiest of sins

Vanity
Unto
Into and onto
Insanity

Come, it's your turn at the mic

The Silver Bullet

Dandelions awaken

"I'm frightened," she whispers
Older and lonelier
Than she ever dreamed
She could be

Crippling Spring
Another season done
A life of inconsequential making

Faking the time of her life
Opening up to
The usual strife

Where flowers blossom
But the scent
Never reaches
Her senses

Dense and world-hardy
Ready to party
Till the break of dawn

Covering up
Porn hits
Which tits
Did well today?

Thine suffering a test
Of foolhardiness
And the Byzantine way
Humans play
Justified in extremes

Little else seems
Comparable to self
When obsession of soul
Makes you lazy

These days it's normal
To be half crazy

And the lines that you find
Are permanently blurred
And are guaranteed
To make you hazy

Perhaps simply choose
To forget
To forget
You'll only regret
Time spent so
Focussing
On the way of things

And your love
Is a silver bullet
Which, truth beknown
Will never ever
Actually save me

The Status Crisis

Taking notes
On the oblivious nature
Of fecundity

Barren city
Crosses over
In night times
Into dream sweats

Stop pressing on me

Your state of things
It's seriously
Distressing me

Yes, there's more to do
More to see
But the threatened state of me
Is overwhelming

As light fades
From the eyes
Of mortals
Around me

And sounds blur
Decibels drowned
In the latest whir
The buzz
The tick
Of a deafening heart

The urban movement
The mass atunement
To a high-rise god

The suggestion
Of man-made creation
Destroying any notion
Of wholeness for all

When once there was hope
Of taking pride in our place

Now it's just a face
A body
A clepto comradery
Stealing each other's
Sense of self
In the hope of accosting
Extreme wealth
At anyone's expense

Whoever has the most
Clearly makes the most sense

As I curl up and cry
Plead to the sky
To the stars and the moon
To rectify this imbalance

To reinstate some semblance
Of soulful normality

Please, before I drown
Swamped by this town
And it's benign artifice
Of pompous social regality

Who Are You Again?

Wettest, dirtiest
I felt it deep down
A national sensation
Down here underground

Feeling strange
I rearrange
Herring to the chorus

Try hard, love
Not to bore us

Delusions of Grandeur

You think you're the chosen one?

Come to me
Sober
Drug free
Your mind on the verge of crazy
And skirting a ring of fire
With a drive that takes you higher
Than narcotics ever could

A life force petrified
Turned to stone
Turned to wood

Do you think you ever could?

Have they ever told you that you should?

A fiery self-destruction
Burning to the ground
Over and over
With the ferocious need
To implode
A super nova
Nothing but
Star dust left
Exploding into
Other dimensions

Yet you fail to mention
That which took you there
For free?
Left to recover
And pay the overpriced fee

For that which you were chosen
for
You still fail to see
Come to me sober
Maybe then we'll see

Fone the Tone

I've got this one thing in my
                pocket
And if I aim it straight I'll rock it
A deeper sense of here and now
A fuck it that will shock it

I shudder when I move
Too old to get in the groove
Setting forth a sturdy pace
As I watch my craft get stooged

The pull of every minute
The hope and expectation
The washing and the dishes
The summoning of a nation

Starseed radiation
Brittle to the bone
Volcanic heart explosion
Don't forget to fone the tone

Ah, Tedium

Can you feel the passion?
I'm making it my mission
To cure this position
Dealing with information
You're delivering en masse

Boring fucking titbits
Feeling like a nit-wit
Summoning up attention
But you need so very much

No such thing as nut shells
Those for whom the toll bells
Ringing in my ear

Dozing off in quarters
Wishing your speech was shorter
Yet something's becoming clear

Eventually I see
It just takes
So fucking long

Let's Get It On

Who gives you your funk?
On cloud nine
Dreamin' of spunk
Licking your chops
Waitin' on the big flop
Hard as a ram
N' bounce all ya can

Then we go slow
And I test you out
Inching in
You moan and shout
Driving your spasms
Slovering your breasts
We engorge your chasms

And when the rhythm's just right
You're looking like
You might die of fright!

But you hold on
And on
And on

And then you're gone
Away and sailing
The smoothest seas

My knees quake then
And my heart aches
To fill you and fulfill you

But your vibrato cries
And lustful sighs
Tell me I got nothing wrong

And I'm seized with the heat
Release in ecstatic defeat
Left to relish
Each time we get it on

Capitalism High

Follow us
We'll show you how to consume
What to buy
When to die
How to live
How to fly

We care about you
How you spend
Your hard-earned cash
Just like hash
What a high

Feeling good
Feeling free
Look what's in
The bag for me

I earned it
How can I spend this money?

Capitalistic virtue
Here we dance
Around the money tree

Questing forth conspiracy
Believing in what's best for me
And equipped with such searing
　　　　intellect

Why these modern values
I continuously reject

There's No Money in Art

How do you spell art?

Does it start with critique?

It used to end in poverty

Gentlemen Behaviour

Gentle rhythm
Of gentlemen behaviour
Young girls look to saviours
Help in their hour of need
Orgasm replete per steed

Nothing like a brother
To make it as your lover
Whipped in cosmic lusting
Trusting first and true

What else can you do
When someone takes you down
Shakes you down
Do I make you frown?

Or was it something already on
your mind?

Never certain what to find
Deep in recesses
Of sex and soul
What is it other lovers know?

I'd give it all
For my afterglow

Lecture Me

Callous moron
Fortitude valley
Spare me what you really think

Quite cleverly you protest
Against the notion of a tigress
And tell me that I stink

As my tail whips
I squit

And you too smell now
Like the art of my devotion

Real Men

Mumbling our maleness into
        corners
No longer topics we once
Would have talked about

Just random
Lifetime servants

Made out to be
So handsome
In our finest
Refinery

Blah blah blah

Eat
Sweet
Relax with a beer
Chill to the max

Why not?
You pay your tax

Show Us Your Tits

My effulgent portrait
Poised with serious head
Carried to dimension
Does my crime deserve your love?

See me from my waist up
Do you desire a taste?
Or is it my imagination?

Do my gimbles make you meow?
Transgression for discretion
Fantastic fantasy fulfilled

For that is what I'm here for
To serve you in this gaze
Sequacious fervent haze

My bosom makes you sparkle
Rebuffing all at once
The notion that you want me
Questioned with sullied truth

Think not my nipples' arousal
'Tis none if not a scree
To purge incondite sentiment
More than tits to thee

My humble birth beginning
Alive with sexual finesse
Condoned in fruitous sentiment
My art has won the day

Justified transition
Comes a long creationist way
And here you keep staring
What more can I say?

1 AM AND ALonE

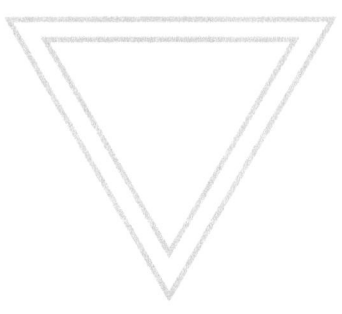

The Exemption

Crafty spokesman
Pomp and tit
Wit so vile
And pile of shit

Delivering spiels of contempt
Ah, you must be exempt
From forest fires lit

Donnie Darko Dissing

I'm longing for this light
I want to feel and taste
Artistic space

Full and fathomed
Drug ritual perspective
Opening opened doors
You've been here before

The ghost of satisfaction
Taunting, whispers
Donnie Darko dissing

Shall I piss in your ear?
Or stand here in fear?

Reminded of laws and love
A push from up above
In the hope of sheer momentum
As long as it's art, baby
Who cares for consequence?

Bested for provision
Group experience decision
Dark and shadowed
Awaiting lighter vibration
Romantic citation
Or haven't you heard?

Involuntary convulsion
Momentary repulsion
Delivery dissention
When ecstasy is the word

Malignant

Purging temptation
Don't want to know
About the past
Rainbow refracts
In the looking glass

Was she sweeter than me?
Her taste more replete
A soft and loving heart
I can't repeat

Master of your desires
And sexual malaise
As you grew closer
Each and every day

Your best friend keeps you
              smiling
Connected to she
But now that's supposed to be me

Don't be jealous
Don't compare
He says to stem my zeal
But what am I supposed to feel?

If I had my way
Shed new skin on this day
Soul mates and lovers
Are memories here to stay

Fuck off apostle
Reflecting a cross over today

Trolls

'Go on, do it,' they whispered
'Spread hate, spread fear'
Cheering her on
To do her worst

But with every venomous word
They lashed her back
Laughing perilously
As the cat-o-nine-tails
Drew trickling blood
From the gory welts

Driving her down
Upon her own sword
Piercing her heart
Slicing her insides

The devilish accord
Of her own foolish hate

Summer Loving

January came and went
And in the end my heart lay spent
Rushing through the pantomime
Hoping it could make you mine

In the end we lost each other
Now I cry without my lover
The seasons dashed what could
        have been
Alive and haunting in my dreams

Dwelling upon
The thrill of touch
When I never thought
I'd feel as much

I came along
Sweet Valentine
Looking for
One more heart's crime

The only way
To build a bridge
My ghost alone
Out on Summer Ridge

A way to feel
The temperature rising
The sun still here
And I'm still surviving

The light, the beats
The holy shrine
So young, so wet
So full of sweat

Ain't even started
Living yet

A smile, it spreads
And deep within
I'm ready to enjoy
This holy sin

When out of the corner
Of my eye
I challenge myself
Not to die

You're holding her
You're moving on
And this is not
My favourite song

Yet rhythm and movement
Harmonise
Above this
I have got to rise

The Relevance of You

Don't touch what's not yours
Get down on all fours
You know I need to borrow the
        light
Oh, alright

Wind's finally in my hair
And I'm all wet
Do I bother caring?
Any call for sharing?

Float away, sounds good to me
Works for serendipity
Mambo shaker, crazy quaker
Graphic noise thrust casually

Omit my mood
You'll figure it out
When I'm not rude
The land is taking me

Bubbles of love keep shaking me

Test it, try it, see if it's new
Expect, react, resist or desist
All markers read to garner your
        bliss

So best decide on your statement
Follow through your lament
Art hearts quiver, shiver and
        strive
And treasure the energy spent

Somewhere, someone's waiting
While you sit around debating
The relevance of you

The Twisted Abyss

> Drowning my thoughts
> In an acidic pool
> Of petrified piss
>
> You're here
> I've got you
> I've seen you
> You're better than this
>
> This twisted abyss
> Where feelings flee
> Leaving thoughts amiss
> You're grounded in the short term
> But you'll soon get the gist
>
> Rock-climb the canyon believing

Pathological Narcissists

To all the tragic
Sadistic
Sociopathic narcissists
In my life
This one's for you

You think you're larger than life
That the world owes you
And you can get away
With any underhanded
Spiteful
Deceitful
And destructive action
That you feel like
Because everyone you've
                charmed

But all your glamour
And sickening conceit
Hides away
The most hideously scarred
And ugly little person
Deep inside

And I feel sorry for you

The Foe

You, you alien fuck

Yeah, I knew what you were
    thinking yeah
Had to believe your intentions
    were sincere
Hell yeah, no choice
And trust is the champion of all
    evils

True to your word, you took me
    in
Felt safe
Safe enough to heed the warning
    signs
And bank it all

Just as the sensual purity of
    intention sways
And heat finds its way to the
    heart

Be
Lend

Of yourself and try to find out
              where
The key is
I understand
I know

Is that what you were thinking
When you pressed yourself into
              me
Warm and pulsing
On a kitchen bench
Some crazy Spring day?

What soft fruit lies beneath this
              scratchy surface?

No
Because here was something new
Old, but a new time

These things take time

And hey, true to her world
Word
Friend, right?
Friend or foe?

Who would know
When you drew me into your lap
To stare me in at will
Such a magic man

Still, I hear your grace notes in
                dreams
Telling me not to feel that way
That's okay
I never did anyway

Not really
No way

I sensed it, I'm not stupid
But I didn't need it
A fraction of time
And a second gone
That's how it was
And too easy to see

Maybe you didn't realise
That your fractions
Could be the sum of me
That you were too blind to see

You need to earn your silence
                with someone

It's funny that you always caught
                me crying
But no, landlord
Your voice ringing in my ear
So bloody loudly
That I didn't feel like answering

Coordinating senses can be a
                melancholy chore
And your psychoanalysis is to me
A bunch of keys jangling

I'll take the ones I need
And quickly unlock the doors
For these lessons I'm grateful
Beyond that nothing more

No Signal

The sign I sent out
On a satellite
Was ignored

Scanning the skies
With the misconception
That the signal
I would receive
Would be believed

My Chunky Life

Time is trickling on
Tickling me here
Whipping me there

Deep welts
Versus heart melts
And I'm frazzled beyond
Words of wisdom

A happy whole donut
Until someone took a bite
Out of my chunky life

Blue Beard

Eat and drink
Cannot think
To stop myself

I have to figure out
How he sways me
How he plays me

He watches me
When he sits
Outside my circle

Sometimes I let him in
I don't mean to
He just comes in

Where should I go
To build my defences?

Devise a plan
To see him safely
To a third quarter
Where his meddling heart
Beats less frantically

None of us need
Be this unhappy

But oh! How he torments me so!
With cigarette ash
And fly spray
Anything to bait my breath

And it works so well
I almost hardly breathe

Decision Time

Clever boy
You have me in your hands
But if you think about it long
        enough
You better tell me where I stand

Times are tough
But I'm still in high demand
And if you keep playing so fucking
        rough
I'll take my chances with the
        shifting sands

C'mon now, enough
Don't tell me who to be
You're the one who's taken so
        much
More than I had to give
You should be laying down your
        life for me

Get it straight
If you somehow think
That I can't make a deal

I am strong
Who are you
To tell me how to feel?

I'm the one
I may come undone
But you need to see
That my heart is still free

It's my heart
And it's free

Ludicrous Expectations

Curled up in a ball
Recoiling from what it is
You just said to me

You bled me
Like a stuck pig
Fiery jig of torture
How can I hurt her
Before she goes away?

Aspiring to be a lady
Instead you cut me
Somewhere in your head
Needing to see me dead
To your world
Of short and swift asunder

Watch me as I blunder
Fucking up
Again and again

And I can't help it
When I'll never be any different

Lacking in measurement
Afflicting soul commitment
Your extreme and ludicrous
Expectations of me

Porn Brain

Disconnect me
Double D
And disaffect me

Trailing all your persuasions
With global limitations

Wondering about
The size of my arse
And whether you
Find it attractive

Worrying about
The state of my brain
As it lies here
Inactive

Just Joshing

Take me into the darkness
Surround me with your fiery
    breath
Strip me bare of all I thought was
    true
Make me into the magic of you

I study you with my finest form
I look for where it is
I might ease my tension
A love too longing to mention

Alas, if all but you knew
The time devoted to you
The obsessed nature of my
    craving soul
My fleshless, hungry, ghostly goal

I want you all for myself
Need to eat you up
Want to fill my chalice with every
    ounce
Of liquid ecstasy drop

You bleed into the night
You give me quite a fright
For I'm on my knees
And if I'm not wrong
This isn't happening right

I gag at your proposal
Useless for all I know will
Deliver little
In return for my heart
Still what happens now will be
                fatal

You brandish your weapon so
                well
And I buckle to the form that you
                meld
As you flatter me some
But offer me none
Of the dreams you know full well
                are real

So I'll fuck you pretending I'm
yours
But my soul just fills up with
these sores
A pustulant sense
Of love gone wrong
New history laid out in scores

Will I ever be able to forgive
How you operate just like a sieve
Letting me through
The best part of you
But with little at the end we can
give

Crippled more with each passing
day
I think of what it is I might say
When the look on your face
Says I'm done and I'm gone
Oh well, just joshing, okay

Maiden, Witch and Crone

    Too old?
    Too young for the times
    Too many things
    You will never understand

    Aah, life is grand

Anti-Christian

Who wants to be the one
To explain things
A million times over?

Again
And again
And again

Destined to fail
In the most spectacular
Of fashions

Dreaming of your own accord
Troubling notions
Facing the fraudulence
The complete lack of endearment
To your horrific sentiment

Tell me again
Why it's all about you?

Why we need to protect ourselves
From all you do
When the worst example
Of humanity

Oh please
Oh more, not more
Especially when
It's plain to see

You've got it in for me

Lost Cause

Oversaturated by staged emotion
The television's on
Just so I don't feel lonely
A regulated sense of if only
Battering at my brain

Consumerist urges
Verge into need
Forgetting to question
This burgeoning greed
That threatens to drive
The nature of me
As I continue to hide
In front of the tv

But it's educational, I reason
Entertaining occasionally
Depending on the season

Yet as hours pass
I'm stuck here fast
Arse glued to this couch
Boasting permanent slouch
The quandary of movement
For food and survival
Yet the pull to return to it
Seems more than just tidal

Can't seem to unhinge
My electronic binge
As my eyes grow
As square as can be
Dreaming dreams
Of roaming out there free

Away from this lost cause of me

The Hoax

Each time I've laid me down to sleep
You've prayed the Lord my soul to keep
But every time you'd have me wake
You'd will the Devil my soul to take

For destiny you would behest
If money was all that we knew best
The thrill bestills romantic will
As long as you can pay the bills

We'll test you by your best accord
When values only reminisce discord
You'd blatantly state your moral view
If cashish comes along with you

Understand, we don't care how
Karma bills the fractions now
Sponsor a child from overseas
While charity bleeds its own disease

I watch and wait here off the
                blocks
Praying I don't end up sucking
                corporate cock
Yet I close my eyes and bid
                disguise
In a world filled with so many lies

Cut the Cord

Get off the nest
Truly beguiled
By life and its tests

Safety condoned
Instead you're atoned
But who are you to argue?

The life that you've shown
Without mummy or daddy
You'd be lost and alone

But that's the whole point

Time Waster

Oh, dear god
Let me be
Somewhere else
Just for a little while

Please, oh please
Take me away
To another place
Another space

You seem to like
Being the demon
That raises heart attack

You like to be the monkey
Etching grazes
On my back

Would you care to be the zombie
To feast on my brains too?
Or are they not to your taste?

Time with you
Feels such a waste

A Cold War in the Global Village

The bitterness of youth
Settles on the dusty shoulders
Of elders alive and spent
In the making of life

The creative device
That was able to connect
And make dreams come true

A magical archetype
That trips up notions
Of who has what power

Beauty sours
In the face of ingratitude
In the space of ugly attitudes
Of entitlement
And the right to attention

Failing to mention
In the parameters of social
        awareness
The space of media sharedness
That time spent is valued

Not perfect but justified

Uncertainty revised
So that every moment counts
And every ounce
Of love given
As time claws out
Is magical and apparent

Devoid of judgement
If you know what's best

Anything less is a falsitude
A fake claim on the drastic
A succumbing to plastic time
To make believe and all pretend
That which pays no dividend

So mock and scoff
Should it be your will
Ridicule so
If it makes you feel superior
And empowered

Any trace of might
That may shower down upon you
On a cold and empty night
In our global village

War of Words

Tsk tsk
It's a war of words
Tsk tsk
Or hadn't you heard

Tsk tsk
Bombs dropped in night times
Tsk tsk
There'll never be a right time

2 AM AND DANCING

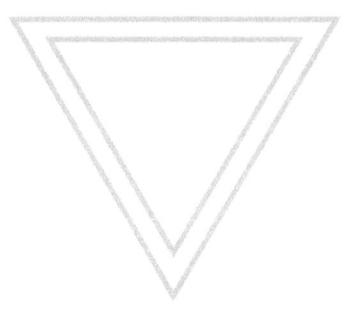

My Way

The raw shell of nothing
Flashed into the night
With a tone of subsidence
And the guilt of no right

But a long, stiff remembrance
With a swift song delight
Is a dance in the memory
And a foraging respite

With a beer in one hand
Flashdancing, no fright
Commanding the passion
Of a thousand in flight

For the scene of enamour
Comes clean and oh so bright
Bereaving no frog net
Freedom's hindsight

The Highways and Byways of Life

Left standing on the highways
          and byways of life
I struggled to fill my role
As an upstanding citizen
For those wanting to own me
And disown me

A role model for who
If I queried the rain
Falling on my head
And the social modelling
That threatened to suffocate

Why, explain to me again
Why I need to fulfill this niche?
Fill this mould?

What fortune untold will it bring
If I struggle daily
Stroking the corporate cock
That promises golden showers
Reaming for so many hours
While the essence of love and art
Fritters away?

Still, you must pay your way,
          that's life

I must pay?
Pay for my life
And somehow to do so
I pay with my life

Well, it's my fault, see
Because if I just believed as others do
If I nested on the biggest mound
Surely the heavens would resound?

Would they take note and reward me
For arduous contribution to industry?
To find me comatose in front of the tv
Hunting and gathering all that comes with a fee

The nature with which I was trained to be
But does it really make me free?

I'm told it does
My will, my way
The way forward
Into another day

To wake and not scream
To live out some dream
Where all that glitters is gold
With riches untold
That tell me I haven't sold out

I couldn't have
I'm toeing the cultural line

Will it all out
Will I get what I want?
Will I leave my mark
As I stumble through darkness
So very bright
Made so
By the artificial light?

Or are they cosmic
The rays that guide my way?

As I fall into the booby trap
And taunt Mother Nature
With the rest of the progressive
           mob
The true way forward
With the view to expand

There's no going back
Cap firmly in hand
Pipe dreams and grand schemes
Fit so well
Into capitalistic measures

So I continue to dig deep
Brush away the tears I weep
As I continue my search for the
           treasure
That mankind was hoping I'd find

Maybe even spell it out for all
In good time

Ladies Don't Fart

Themes of my lifetime
That I'm boring you with
Casually
But you don't know me
You don't know me

Once beaten and deflated
See how long I've waited
To feel alive again

What is a friend anyway
If not a hound to be haughtened
Quite regularly

Faithfully quipping
Territorial shitting
We finally stink the same
Only farting is not your game
And I'm full of it

When I said your love
Carried me on the wind
The smell not so sweet as we first
        thought?

Touching dagger of stench bombs
Fired in your direction
Ripping at the heart of moment
Your honesty does me proud
And we cover new ground again

You smell just like my friend

The Matriarch

Do I detect a note of nastiness
In that concerned tone?
Repeatedly transparent apparel
Your Emperors' Clothes conceit

Stuns me there's anything to do
Around and about the likes of you
When I've given more
Than I ever had to give
Ever could before

Never to make the same mistake
Entrust to you my life
To have it filled with strife

Subliminal sunboat strickening
Pay to be less sickening

If the cuff would seem
Not to be seen
And suffer far less screening

The river has me thinking
Winding
Twisting

And so do your words

Waiting

Bask and baste
Mask gone to waste
As you crust me out with your demon
Not letting me suck on your semen
Genuine with reason
But I just can't with the here and now

My frustration grows
And the stampede shows
How little there is
To relieve with
When I'm wanting you
And nothing else

Belching at stars
And begging indifference
To endure this resistance
My dying heart subsistence
Don't leave me in this state
Only time can make me wait

But you have the means to free me

State the Obvious

Jealousy spoken
Tokens applaud
Relatively vehement
Whilst acting bored

Trumped up on trivial
The dance of the divine
Stop worrying
Love what you have
Not that which you cannot

It's bleedingly convivial, really

The Asp

Your job is to pass on wisdom
and regard
Not venom and thunder

Always Was, Always Will Be

Where is Australia?
Is it in my heart?
Is it in your gut?
Is it in your ear?
Cause all I hear
Are watered-down truths

You build it up
And burn it down
Abandoning the heart
Of each small town

The land as she cries
And her people that die

Staking our claim
Making our name
On a global stage
The new take
On the noble savage

Chewing her up
Spitting her out
Divvy up her market shares
While we decide what we're
about

As Uluru calls
And Jim Jim falls
Black blood boils
For the love

The true heart
Of whose country?

Wild Woman

Comfort me, I'm blue
Trapped by my derision
Pretending only word

Account my inner vision
Too cowardly to share
Honestly, I'm shy
No self-belief to dare

Crumbling
I need you, Wild Woman

I have no desire
To inspire my thoughts
When all of your lessons
Amount to naught

With every mind
I try to tell of you

Winter is Coming

>We wail out of tune
>We harmonise and bastardise
>We rape and torture
>Like Vikings with the final say
>
>The machinations of this land
>As commodity

The Bends

Talking your way
Through anti-depressants
When apparent borders
Seem far less incessant

Building up dreams
And vision that seems
To craft the juggling
Of dealing with presence

What is this thick skin?
The light becomes so suddenly
        dim
Questing forth our juggernaut
To solidify the trends

But we're breathing hard
And your confident start
Is giving me the bends

Holed up in this pit
Covered in so much shit

Your sympathy symposium
Is sickening to the core
Bearing me no practical use
And levelling me no score

Can you be my emotional crutch?
Or could I never hope as much?

By the by
Can only try
To fritter the fretting away

But in the cold light of day
In my shell I may always stay

The Outskirts

She existed
On the outskirts of your mind
Filling you with plenty
Snared in her web

So you sent her along
To write you a song
But by the time she was done
You'd already moved on
Adamant you're not the kind
Who should be kept waiting

She bated her breath
And sated her loft
She crept up the crevice
Carrying a degree
Of artistic measure

And somewhere up high
She hoarded her treasure
Defining it all
On the inside

Like any that grew
How well they all knew
Or so they liked to believe

Should any care
It was decided then and there
As the wheels spun around
The sound far too great
For many to bear

Still loathe for inconsistency
She got the gist
But the force kept them bound
And tethered

Fuck Off, Ho

How would you feel
If I came to you
Shoved my tits in your face
Said my sex you'll never erase?

For I fucked your man
A thousand ways from Sunday
And in the lazy haze
Of lovers' gaze
I dreamed him into dimensions
That you will never reach

And each time that you came
        hither
I sent him a warm-blooded shiver
To remind him of all
Of the love that stands tall
As we ship's sail into sunsets
That your life could never let

Destined to be helpless
Lack of love so reckless
Never to know the sensuousness
Of how it was for me

And while my bosom bounces
And your self-confidence flounces
How trite you will seem
Forever wishing your dream

But only in your pants will you
        cream

As you sliver falsely over solution
Your sex and desire execution
Shall never fulfill your dilution

So go on and crave
But your life you may save
When my man finally stops being
        your delusion

Only the Strange

Questing forth the inexperience of
    the night time
Shedding dreams in the right
    frame of being incensed
Cleverly devout and nary a test
Stitching together all you can
    believe
You always try to make me leave

Throwing in your daggers
Your heart and mind trap
    swaggers
Differencing the pleating
Of berate and lullaby

Trials and tribulations
Inflated situations
Streaming download persistence
A case of relative resistance

Jesus me my cross
Fill my empty time frame
And blame me
Just blame me

Go the fuck ahead and shame me

While you're at it, derange me
The estrangement of one who
        seems so strange

The Time Has Come

All this time spent sitting tight
Now I clasp the hand of fate
How could I keep waiting
After this?

After all I've longed for
Comes knocking on the door
Demanding I step up
And challenge the score

I've settled, I know
Wanting so much
Never knowing which way to go
To really fulfill this dream in me

Believing it could be real
But treating it like a fantasy
Nothing I could ever
Take seriously

Yet here's a chance
As the gods will me forth
Into a universal dance
Where dreams
Can become reality

Life demands
That much more from me
In worlds I thought
I'd never see

I have to work, have to try
So crazy to ever let this pass me
          by
When there must be a reason
A new time, a season

Where everything I could be
Will mean that much more

Cellular Bomb-times

If I tell you a secret
Will you listen?

If I show you my heart
Will you balk?

Counting numbers and figures
The electronic way we now talk

You reach me
Through cellular bomb-times

Bloom

Cover me in roses
Penetrate me
With a thousand
Innocuous poses

The height of self-interest
Is blooming

Humble Pie

It looks like you're going
To wreck me again
You don't really see me
Do you?

I come along
Reeking of
My own significance
With only love
And good will

And you think you're humble

The Urban Addict

Look at you
Acting like it's fine
Stopping the thinking of rhyming
Troubled by emotionless timing

The intensity of your presence
And the way
You're always trying to use it
To your advantage

Crowding into urban spaces
Falling in lust with so many faces
Crawling back to the wasteland
The deserted inner landscape
That you call home

Close Your Eyes

Looking for the something
Not with you
But beyond you

That which
You do not even know
That you have

Because one day
You least expect
But you wished it all the same

You willed it with your weakness
You fed it with your bleakness

Shocked and dumbfounded
The shadows are bleeding
The creatures are needing

They want to give you
What it is you seek

Little did you realise
The dream you harbour
The frivolous notion
Of little consequence

Would be the nuclear explosion
To disrupt your very essence
And you thought never
Could it be

How could it happen to me?

I'll tell you
If you want
Otherwise
Close your eyes
And pulsate
The pulverizing potion
Of your fears

This may take years

The Frozen Heart

Ah me
Who'd have thought
The son of a sociopath
Would be who
My significant other
Would turn out to be?

A wild and free spirit
Seemingly untamed
Until you tether
To the legacy of your name
Then they've got us by
The short and curlies

Freeze
Freeze your heart
Freeze your mind
Freeze your spirit
Just stay still
Do nothing
Cop the ill-will
And play along

Once we get out of the blinding
glare
Of their spotlight
We can go back to normal

Nothing about this
Is remotely fucking normal

Denied

Bright lights
Flicker then fade
Plunging darkness
Crab-walking blind

Don't touch me
Just look
Drink me in
My holy essence

My hot sex
Burns your eyes
And leaves you wanting
More

Flounder at the thought
Salivate
But you'll never know
Never be sure

Hail the Greedy

    Crocodile footpaths
    The space where
    Greedy men
    Hoard concepts
    Of value

    But value little

Get Away

Radiant hearts that aspire
Feelings that cut so close to the
wire
Corrupting the worst of my
sensibilities

How 'bout you get the fuck away
from me?

Don't Leave

Tony the bird

Only the brave

The Devil Grins

Strange days
And plays
Of suffering surfaces

You know not of
Have not been to
Could not seem to care
In the share
Of a grand holden dare

The leaf that turned
And the new day dawned
Relief in a slaughtering nuisance
Of crippling essence

Born to shout down
In a blaze of glory

Gory
Garish
Political pipelines
Times are changed
And the record set

Haven't got
The best of them yet

Treading on filters
And truth that seems
To brandish a herring
Million dreams

Brush teams off
To see who wins
And copulate all
For a thousand sins

Clean up fate
And childish spins
When the blood finally settles
And the devil grins

Tempted to Hate

I wish I had
A big, luscious dick
That I could fuck you with

I wish the muck with which
I fill my life
Helped me feel
Alive and free
Instead of trapped
And barely breathing

I wish the seething way
He stares at me
Would return upon the opponent
Perfection of his own body
So that he could eat
His own pound of flesh
And feast upon
His own regret

The temptation to hate
And to constantly hurt
May just be
A habit that I've learnt

But I've withstood
Every fucked up scene

That's threatened to crush
Me and my dreams

So who the fuck are you
To rain on my parade?

Tickertape falling
Like faery dust
And that which must
Be tended to

I live so far beyond
The likes of you

With your pretty boy looks
And narcissistic needs
So deep in the shallows
You're caught up in reeds

You'll never be free
Your lack of grace
And one day it'll hit you
Like a punch in the face

That you wasted so much energy
Hating those that you deem
Beneath you
And your corporate dream

Your cash to splash
The fashion of your heart
Empty, hollow
No room to grow
Into anything remotely
Caring or wise

And I'll see it all written
In the stars of your eyes
As they dull and you fall
Unknowing and blind
Finally ready to learn
The depths of your time

And no doubt
I'll pity you
And show you kindness still

Because that is the oneness
That is universal will

Potty Mouth

Just because I talk like a sailor
Doesn't mean I won't fuck like a
siren

3 AM AND COMING HOME

The Call of Nature

Bring on the nightshift
Let your heart slip
As you close the door
And lock yourself in

The wind is calling
In ancient tongues
Tales of fire and passion
As we roll into one

Creating a union
The powers that be
Offer cosmic delights
While you watch your tv

Fighting the feeling
You've been here before
Your country is calling
Open the door

Last Night

Last night
I felt I knew you

Last night
In a drunken haze
I felt a moment
Of clarity

I looked deep
Into your eyes
And I saw a place
Carved out
Just for me

Inside of you
With me

Last night
You held my hand
Held my stare
Held my heart

Last night
I knew nothing else
Except you

Now every night
Reminds me
Of last night

Men

What a ruse
What a by-line
What a headline

"Great set of tits"

H'WHAT!

You heard me
It's art
Have a heart, bitch

And asp is such a common word

The Shit Heap

It's as though
You're sitting
On a shit heap

You fly off
To buzz around
Looking for other shit
Telling yourself
'This is okay
I like this
I'm happy with this'

But inside
You're perfectly aware
Nesciently so
That in essence
Your life
Is a pile
Of shit

And when you're ready
To see this
You will be that fly
Trapped in the bottom
Of a big glass
Buzzing around
Unable to fly out

Dying
With the resonance
Of your own buzz-style death-cry
Pounding down in your ears

Buzz little fly, buzz away
Buzz off and don't bother me

The Chopper

Weapons of mass decimation
Offended by nature's creation
Don't rob me of the satisfaction
The undoing of your whole life's
dedication

Jealous Jeans

Pizza daze
Ferment my drive
Jealous jeans
Have a funny walk

Balking at the moonlight
With an enigmatic flair
Looking up isotopes
Magnesium arthroscopes

Open your mouth
And say too much

Your rush will be along soon

Love's a Peach

Love
It's a peach, huh?

What is love?
A beautiful face?
A perfect sing-song voice
And an enigmatic presence to
        support it

A broken heart, whose owner
When impressionable
Was never provided the skills
To recover from it

A heart, pulverized
Smashed to smithereens
Whose natural course to
        regenerate
Formed the most intensely
        negative charge
As to allow the owner
Without any apparent will
To be drawn
Magnet-like
To a contender
Whose own heart
Has enough positive charge
To see them through
Their own survival
When the other is irrevocably
        forced
To commit its atomic creation

It will happen like this
Someone will always come off
Second best
The other left less battle scarred

The ashes of a broken heart
Are the gun powder
That loads an oppressor's pistol
The vision of which
Is a gun pointed
Straight for you

Maybe they're trigger happy
Maybe it's new for them
To brandish such a weapon

Maybe you should see this
And step out of the way

The Shallows

I held her stare
In the forequarters of my mind
At risk of all and none
Around me

Their words foolish
Underscored
By a shallow fear
That keeps them wading
And never knowing

Last night
There were few of us learning
But oh, how we!

Words
Failure

Me, who holds the glass dagger
Sinking deep into the heart
That bleeds so perishably
Left wounded and weeping
For all to see

None to feel
How to heal
How to give without feeling

Fraudulence
Petulance
Distance
Resistance

When the War Finally Ends

If I steal time
Will I pay for it?

Will it haunt me
Like an old memory
That was woken up too early?

Exploding its myth
All over me
In a chaotic context
Like a German soldier
Questioning his time and place

Who cannot ever erase
That which he must do
To find his way back to you

Grabbing whatever he can
That doesn't slip through his
              fingers
Or sliver icily over his soul

I will make it my goal then
To believe in the best
Rainbows and stars
Till the war finally ends

Pain put to rest
Then I'll steal no more

Time

Time is passing
Time heals all wounds
But time
Is all you have

Are you lonely
With no one
By your side?
In your bed?
In your life?

No one to share
In your glory days
Your great life moments

No one who isn't drunk
As drunk as you

Do you think about your life
With all that time to spare?
Are you filled with remorse
When time forces you to think
           about
All the shitty things you've done?

Are you sorry?
Do you ever want to ring me
And say so?

To grovel and beg forgiveness
To make amends
Before it's too late?

Probably not

But remember this
Before the guilt
Finally kicks in
And you're riddled
With a sense of loss
And self-loathing

That time waits
For no man
Especially not
Someone like you

The Takeaway

No perfect start
To achieve some perfect end
Send me your love
But not your pity

I lived in your city

It wasn't clean
It was noisy and dusted
Feelings rusted up
Under a broken lock and key

Do y'all speak for me?
Did you even hear my language?
I speak in tongues so refined
They only whisper their invisible
               touch

How much can you learn
Before you see it my way?
All I see is the highway

Why should I settle
For any less?
Don't tell me
Your life's no mess

Share the shambles carelessly
Then ask me
To paint you a picture

A pretty one?

Where is the light?
Gone-gagged by red flight
But price is commanded
And I'll pay
Yes, I'll pay

Then I'll pray
For the heart and soul
I know to be true

Life just never asked
That I be close to you

So save face
And turn the key
This is as honest
As I can be

Portray

Too arrogant for you
Too near to the flame
I can't protect you
Unless you stay

Who would've done
Until you flay
A perfect sunset
No other day

Around the sound
Of familiar ground
The portrayal of deuce-coup
You nuisance troupe

Believe it
Fuck off
Portray

Black Dog Blues

She addresses the paper
As though it were her God
Searching for answers
Unsure of what she wants to
 know

Defeat and selective
 acknowledgement
Rule half of her kingdom
And she lets him down so often

The truth is hard to face

She takes her place
In the chair in the corner
And quietly contemplates
Knowing not what else to do
In these troubled times

She's done scanning the room
Wandering from this to that
Tired of looking for relief in the
 little things
When no longer can it be done

She will sit still and reflect
                inwards
On the only thing that can hold
                her concentration

Her hurting soul
Her bleeding heart
Her aching body

She has grown accustomed
To the awkward desperation
That meeting with other bodies
                brings

Whilst she longs for the company
                of others
She knows that the static around
                her
Drives them away

People are troubled by her
Disturbed literally
In their comfortable or neutral
                zones

Why is this girl so scared?
Why does she behave so
                strangely?

She doesn't really know what
        they're thinking
What makes them move on
They probably don't know
        themselves

It's the way she looks
That's the hardest part
She looks fine!
She even looks great
This girl with so much going for
        her

And so she tries

She carries on like the blades in
        her gut aren't real
She patterns over her buzzing
        head
Collating enough material
To carry out a halfway normal
        conversation

If she can just get past the
                preliminaries
Maybe she's found an ally
A consort
An acquaintance
Maybe even a saviour, if she
                hopes hard enough

No, it's not meant to be
It's never meant to be
Not these days
Months, more than a year now
Since all this fear became so real

She needn't cast her mind back
It's already there, zipping about
Furiously trying to sort out
All the places
Where she went wrong
To get her here, to this point
This endless, dragging point
That she can't seem to get past

If someone could look inside her
See the hurt and pain
Maybe it would go away

Truth was, she had always been a
                bit of a loner
A bit of a fringe-dweller
She'd had friends too, good
                friends
She missed High School
It was the last time she
                remembered
Having a lot of fun

She could be pretty funny
When she had an audience, one
                that she loved
But that was all awhile back now

Seeing herself sitting idly in a
                chair
Letting minutes slip by
She is suddenly struck
By a bout of guilt

It burns up her stomach like acid
Her thoughts start racing
As she tries to imagine
What she could do

Where she could project her
energy
So she wouldn't feel so lazy?
Something that could satisfy her
soul

It weighed heavily on her not
having work
She felt the burden it presented to
her independence
She felt her esteem wane
She felt the fear that grew
With each new day
That dragged her further and
further away
From any place that matched
The description of 'job'

She knew
As all the doctors
Family
And 'concerned' onlookers
Attested to
That the helplessness
Was all
In her mind

All in anyone's mind

She also knew
That with each mounting day
As they were prone to being
That things became
More helpless

The fear was alive in her
Burning her up
It was crippling
Paralysing
Draining her
Of all her energies

How could she possibly
Commit to a job
When this was so real?

She felt sick

She'd asked doctors about this
        feeling in her stomach
She thought maybe they'd have
Some kind of medicine
To help her
Surely it was possible

Most of them passed over it
Like it was something that wasn't
 real
How was it possible
They didn't know what she
 meant?

One counsellor had called it
'Running on empty'

So where do you go when you're
 empty?

Sitting in the chair, she feels tired
But it's not sleepy tired
She picks herself up
And lumbers onto the bed
Allowing the exhaustion to
 consume her

But not before she has time
To remind herself
What a waste of time and space
Her life is

If only she could figure out
What she would really love to do
What she'd be good at
Then she'd have a reason to 'live'

She'd be able to stop putting off
And start doing

Wearily, in her head
She begins to toss over
All the things she could 'do'

She likes to sing
Maybe she could be a singer?
Drawing?
She could be an artist

But for every suggestion she
              makes
A voice pounds her hope
Into submission
Telling her straight
'You haven't got what it takes'

She feels herself coming
To a complete circle
And knowing she's back
To the same lost and lonely place
She can't take anymore

Her body starts wracking
As the cries emanate
From so deep inside of her
That she pleads with the gods
With anyone
To help her

To save her
From her own wretchedness

Far beyond
The brink of exhaustion
She collapses into sleep

It is by no means comforting
And when she wakes
She will feel guilty
For having wasted the time
That she wouldn't have known
How to use anyway

But for now, she escapes
And she revives some

She will wake up
She will live and breathe again
For today

For another day
When she'll finally be able
To look back
And it will all be
A bad dream

The Smiling Assassin

Do you care
To shift upon
This disrepair
Twisting me into dimensions
I struggle to return from

Healthy battlement
Beleaguered by
A wave of resentment
A dizzying spell
Of criminal arrest
A hank laid in my tracks

Do I choose to set sail
Or continue to wail?

A mortal coil
Laced with disgrace
As truth gathers on me
Like a ghost in my face

Dribbling a toxic protestment
Leaking from my gut
My body condoning this rut
As my mind continues to strut

And all the while
You just smile
Discordant tones
Triggering in my bones

Teasing me into transition
Beseeching a nuclear fission
To help me along on my mission
But it can't hide your derision
Or the triggering confusion

A frown set deep
Behind those bright eyes

Will You Marry Me?

Quipped to the eyeballs
Wanting to see
Having it close
Yet needing to be

Heeding the love
Still holding the key
If you'd told me at all
Would I ever be free?

Trapped in a cycle
Grossly concede
If having your approval
Means less energy

Buying the lifelines
And gripping to motion
Crafting the stemmed accord
Whilst flaying your ocean

I apologize
For disturbing your life
Bringing me in
None as a wife

But little is done
If not with some pain
So while I let go
I'll learn to refrain

For presence is courtship
Marriage is scree
If never a convergence
Maybe a plea

Soul Man

    I try and try
    Again and again
    To believe so much
    In the soul of men

Your Choice

A sight to behold
The truancy of gold
The smell of a halfpipe
The songs of old

New worlds disdain
You can barely refrain
And why not, you're talented too
As you cry out in the rain

You could do but you do not
Instead rotting here in the pot
Cooking your goose, setting far
            too loose
But it is your choice, is it not?

Soul Doubt

    Cloud-like, blue stripes
    Spirit and blood
    The lefting motion
    Of spilling into the drain

    Model train
    Spout pouring
    Your heart, my heart
    Which start?

    I thought you might say it
    When you play again
    I would stay again
    If I thought you were truly my
            friend

The Tainted Ones

Bring me into your life
I'll be your monster
To prove all your theories
About who you are

Attract me to your world
So I can dance your tango
A box step that starts
And ends in a circle

Call me forth
To teach you a lesson
To compound your pain
Drive you insane

Count on me
To be the one
Who'll screw you over
Not for fun
But because there's nothing
Else to be done

After all
We are the tainted ones

Stop, Thief

Like a thief in the night
He comes to me
Creeping, crawling
Stealing himself
Into my world

By night
He sees my body writhe
He feels my restless spirit
Watching as I fall
Into the depths of sleep

There is no peace
Not for me
Not while he's here

Like no other man
He comes again
Night upon night

Sifting
Shifting through
My scattered thoughts
Offering little in return
For my broken dreams

I scream
Deafening silence
Piercing my soul

Defeated
Drained
Desperate
For one drop of love
To compensate this madness

I turn
I cry
I run toward
Anything I can find
To relieve this pain

It's still the same

Nothing has changed
Only time
Time remains

I awake to find him waiting
Seeking
Falling
Healing himself
In my world

I am not free
There is no peace
Not for me

Not while he's here

The Inbred Catastrophe

Ripples of solitude
Eking out direction
To be here
In this empty bracket of knowing

Sharing something
And the rain comes forth
Begging indifference
Of a different kind

Culture refining
Stating the obvious
It's a single social solution

Profusely kept
In inept glory
Because my story is hidden
In a different way

How shall we say
And dance to Botany Bay
Leaving chemical intrusion
In toxic capacity

What has to be
The strangest phenomena
Right here
In Australia

An inbred catastrophe
Where ruptured hearts and minds
Toil if you like

And if you don't
Go to hell
Right now

Karmic tale tells
With broken commandments
Sand swept and warm

Can you tell from this
I'm coming home?

Bye Bye Baby

Bend me back
I won't crack
Play to win
One more sin

A dubious night's counsel
What will this ounce do
To the life inside of you?

Who knew
You said no
What to show
At the knife's end

Just blend, honey
Just blend

It wasn't meant to be

I Said No

A conscious movement
A big footstep
In the general direction
Suddenly seems perfection

Wrenched away
With frail redemption
From the sensation
Of dissention

So much malintention
Of love
The fitting dilemma
Permanently scarred

From a lack of consent

Strange Bedfellows

What strange bedfellows we are
Waiting for the moonrise
Pointing out stars
In the night sky

What lifetime is this?
When once we'd have sailed seas
Trekked to remote villages
Sought adventure over hill and
           dale

You don't buy me flowers for
           birthdays
You don't shower me with gifts
But the heavenly arraignment of
           your affection
Hits its mark so swiftly

We hit home runs
And run the home
We've made together

There's no talk of forever

Only the one day
The one time
The each prime moment
We mark on any given timeline

Wronging each other
And longing for each other in turn
The stern way I redress
And you redress me

We make love like a factory
Boiling over and greasing it up
Synchronisation of machinations
And the product is perfect

We work hard for this
We make this thing brand new
And I'll do it for you
Till my dying day

Isn't that what they say?

Weirdo

Remember that time
Ferret boy
So full of energy
Boisterous and excited
To the point of psycho

And everyone thinks your weird

Guns Are Fucked
(But Not as Fucked as the Assholes That Kill People With Them)

Fuck me
Is it really
So awesome
To own guns?

Does it define you?
Empower you?
Enable you somehow
To be the something
Of a vicious
Violent
Killing machine
Within the bounds
Of your best and worst dreams?

Do you want to know what it's
        like
To kill a man?

Do you want to hold the hand
Of a wounded being
Riddled with bullet holes
Guts
And flesh
And bones
And brains
Splattered everywhere
And this is cool?!

What the living fuck!
What the fuck is your story?!

How the hell
Do you ever
EVER
Live to become
A human fucking entity
Who could abide by
Some weapon of choice
Tearing apart, nay
EXPLODING apart
The very essence
The touch
The pumping heart
The bleeding like a stuck pig
The gore of another human being?

Every drop of blood
Every gram of flesh
Are these not precious?

Who the fuck are you
To rail against
Any single one
Of God's designs?

Get the fuck off of
Your mental
Unstable
Unable to see
The cursed reality
Of what you're doing
When you take out
Your pathetic rage
To the point of allowing
Another to die
At your hands
And your fucking insecure
Better be sure
Cause there is no cure
Once you've killed someone
Sense of being

Cause if you don't
And the cure for you
Is what you do
When you feel some relief
Acting out the grief
When you can't outrun
Or hide from
So many wounded hearts
When you steal
Rob from
Rip apart
Obliterate
And completely destroy
The love
The dreams
The connections
Of so many wounded hearts
That you were the cause of

Then fuck you
You complete and utter
Cunt of a thing

If you can't sort your shit
Then I hope life fucks you
Right up the ring

So go ahead
And sing your pathetic excuses
Your white noise
When the ghosts haunt you
And steal your voice

We are all goddam human
And you have a fucking choice

The Expert

I'm an expert in tears
In the years it takes
To heal
To make things better

With happenstance
And love
And hope
And faith

Watch it burn, let it heal for the Gundungarra

Acknowledgements

I'd like to give thanks to Australia's First Nations people, for their care and love of this amazing, grand island, for the power of their culture, and for having the strength and resilience to survive and thrive in the face of Invasion in all of its heinous, evil, despicable forms. My heart flies to every Indigenous person that feels the flow of the ancient history of this land through their blood. I mourn the horror they have collectively suffered and I pray for healing, that all of the mobs of this nation may continue to flourish and help heal country. Always was, always will be.

I'd like to thank my bullies! I have no desire to name these people and I'm not particularly grateful for all that I suffered at their hands before I was able to find the strength to protect myself from them, but I am grateful for the journey that bought me to the place where I was able to connect with that inner-strength, which helped me to grow and become the person I am today. And let's face it, the pen is mightier than the sword! I'm grateful that their disgraceful behaviours gave me so much to write about!

Once again I owe a debt of gratitude to IndieMosh – Jenny, Debbie and Ally, such a dream team to help through this process of bringing my work to life and onto the published page, they are a writer's dream come true. Thank you for making the journey such a wonderful one.

Thanks especially to my little community of Consiton, the Cono mums, the school, the amazing women and men that I've met and the network of families and all of my children's friends, it's been such a joy to be a part of this gorgeous, lively community!

Thanks to Steve of Quest Books in Figtree, and Michael of Garden Lounge Creative Space in Newtown for their support of my work. I'd also like to thank the Two Trees Talking artist community in Wollongong to this end also.

To anyone who's bought any of my books and has spared a kind word for it, I thank you the most! Without you I'm no one, just a dreamer blowing puff and smoke about all of my strange and confronting ideas – thank you for helping make my dreams come true!

About the Author

Catherine Harford is an artist, poet and writer living in Wollongong, south of Sydney, Australia, with her husband and her two children. Wollongong is Dharawal Country, the traditional lands of the Dharawal people and she honours their nation, both past, present and future.

She produces a variety of art, which includes music and video production as well as her penchant for drawing and painting. She has travelled and lived extensively throughout Australia, and she draws on this experience for much of her inspiration when she writes and makes art. She is the published author of the non-fiction work "They Gave Me Truth" and the collection of poems, "Under Moon and Sun" and "American Creek."

www.ingramcontent.com/pod-product-compliance
Lightning Source LLC
LaVergne TN
LVHW040053080526
838202LV00045B/3605